WHAT MAKES
VEHICLES
SAFER?

KAREN LATCHANA KENNEY

LERNER PUBLICATIONS ◆ MINNEAPOLIS

TO MY DAD: THE ANSWER MAN AND THE FIRST PERSON TO TELL ME HOW MY CAR WORKS

Content consultant: James Freudenberg, Director, Master of Engineering in Automotive Engineering, University of Michigan

Lerner Publications Company
A division of Lerner Publishing Group, Inc.
241 First Avenue North
Minneapolis, MN 55401 USA

For reading levels and more information, look up this title at www.lernerbooks.com.

Main body text set in Caecilia Com 55 Regular 11/16
Typeface provided by Linotype AG.

Library of Congress Cataloging-in-Publication Data

Kenney, Karen Latchana, author.
   What makes vehicles safer? / by Karen Latchana Kenney.
      pages cm. — (Engineering keeps us safe)
   Audience: Ages 9–12.
   Audience: Grades 4 to 6.
    Includes bibliographical references and index.
    ISBN 978-1-4677-7913-5 (lib. : alk. paper)
    ISBN 978-1-4677-8652-2 (EB pdf)
    1. Motor vehicles—Safety measures—Juvenile literature. 2. Safety factor in engineering—Juvenile literature. 3. Engineering—Juvenile literature.
    I. Title.
   TL242.K46 2016
   629.04028'9—dc23   2014041108

Manufactured in the United States of America
1 – VP – 7/15/15

CONTENTS

SAFETY ON THE MOVE

Watch the news and you're bound to see some scary headlines. Mid-ocean plane crashes, runaway trains, and deaths from car crashes are the top stories. Major events like these attract attention and readers. That can often mean more advertising dollars for news sources. Social media spreads the news of these tragedies to all parts of the world in an instant. Modern people are bombarded with bad news. So it's easy to understand people's fears about traveling.

But despite the headlines, these kinds of accidents are very rare. Only about eleven out of one hundred thousand people die from motor vehicle accidents each year in the United States. And you're more likely to die from accidental poisoning than from a plane crash! We just don't hear about all the safe journeys that happen every day.

Accidents often show the weaknesses of vehicles. Accidents also show the ways that people can be hurt. But new designs can solve many problems. Better engineering helps prevent crashes. It also helps people survive tragic events. Design improvements make disasters less likely to happen. Planes land perfectly, and boats reach their ports. Trains deliver their cargo, and people drive their cars to work. And many people survive crashes too—all thanks to good engineering!

News reporters seek out disaster stories because scary headlines get people's attention. A story about someone driving a car home safely probably wouldn't make the news!

FIGHTING LOCKUP

It's a rainy night, and the roads are slippery. Your dad suddenly sees a deer and slams on the brakes. The car's tires lock, meaning they stop spinning. And instead of stopping, your family's car slides across the wet road. Then it spins out of control. It's a scary situation, but carmakers have designed something that helps. It's the antilock braking system (ABS). It stops wheels from locking and saves lives.

Before ABS, drivers had to pump the brakes to keep them from locking. Pumping means to quickly press and release the

The ABS helps cars slow down and stop safely on wet or icy streets.

brake pedal several times. But sometimes people slammed on their brakes in a panic and forgot to pump. In modern cars, though, sensors can tell when a wheel is locking. They signal the ABS.

Brakes use a fluid. This fluid is released into tubes. These tubes connect with parts near the wheel that hold the brake pads. The pressure from the fluid squeezes the pads against the wheels.

When the ABS takes over, the brake lever shudders under the driver's foot. The ABS pumps the brake fluid on and off for the wheel that has locked up. This pumps the brakes on that wheel. The wheel starts to slow down, but the car does not spin out of control. The driver can safely steer through a wet patch of road or around an object in the car's path.

When a driver pushes a car's brake pedal, brake fluid is released. The fluid pushes the wheel's brake pads against the spinning wheels to slow them down.

AIR BAG CHEMISTRY

When there's a crash, your car comes to a very sudden stop.
But your body doesn't—it keeps moving forward. If your head
hits the car's windshield or dashboard, you can be seriously
injured. Air bags soften the blow and help save lives. They use
chemistry to inflate in a fraction of a second.

A car has sensors at its front near the engine. When an
impact occurs, it sets off the sensors. They send an electric
signal to a canister that contains a chemical called sodium
azide. The signal causes heat to ignite the chemical. The heat
makes the chemical's molecules break down. One product of
this reaction is nitrogen gas. A small amount of sodium azide
produces 18 gallons (67 liters) of gas. This gas quickly fills a
bag at the center of a steering wheel or on the dashboard. The
air bag then cushions the impact of your head. It absorbs the
forward energy of your body.

A NEAR ACCIDENT

In 1952, John W. Hetrick had a near accident
in his car. It got him thinking: What could be
done to soften an impact for people inside a
car? About a year later, Hetrick got a patent
for his idea of a cushion that could be inflated
if a car suddenly slowed down. But it took
many more years to come up with an air bag design that worked. Early
designs used compressed air, but that can easily catch fire. And some
air bags harmed passengers rather than helped them. Carmakers began
putting air bags in some cars in the early 1970s, although drivers did not
have much interest. This safety feature did not truly catch on until the
1990s. Since 1998, US law has required that all new cars have air bags.
In this photo, a young girl tests out a new air bag design in 1977.

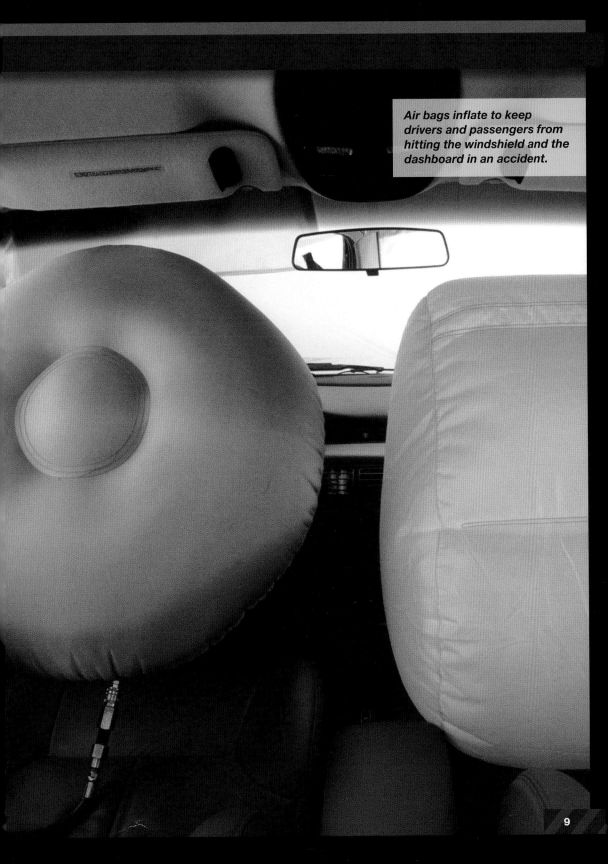

Air bags inflate to keep drivers and passengers from hitting the windshield and the dashboard in an accident.

THE CRUMPLE ZONE

Have you ever seen a car after a bad crash? It probably didn't look much like a car anymore. Its crushed body is the result of energy transfer.

Speeding cars have a lot of motion energy. A body in motion usually stays in motion. The only way it can stop is if an outside force acts upon it. A gradual force, like that caused by brakes, slows a car down. But a sudden force can crush a car. That's because energy never disappears. It just transfers from one form to another.

People can be seriously hurt by the energy of a crash. That's why cars are designed to crumple. The front and the back of a car crumple to absorb a crash's energy. Those parts are called the crumple zone. A rigid cell made from strong steel surrounds the passenger area, like a safety cage. By the time the crash's energy reaches the passenger cell, much of the energy has been absorbed. Less force acts upon the passengers. This helps protect drivers and riders from harm.

A CAR'S SAFETY REGIONS

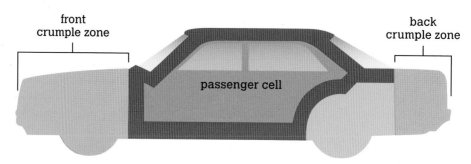

front crumple zone

back crumple zone

passenger cell

MADE BY MERCEDES-BENZ

Engineer Béla Barényi designed the crumple zone. In 1951, he received a patent for his design. Barényi worked for German carmaker Mercedes-Benz. This carmaker was the first to use the crumple zone design in a production car. The first car series with this safety feature was the Mercedes-Benz 1959 W111 "fintail."

The front crumple zone of this car was crushed when it hit a post. Because the front of the car was designed to crumple on impact, the passenger cell mostly kept its shape.

MOVING MAPS

Pilots once used paper maps to find out where they were going. While that mostly worked, paper maps cannot show recent changes. A plane's position cannot be shown on a paper map either. Pilots had to use many tools to figure out where they were on the map.

Digital maps are always up to date. They can show the latest changes, such as new buildings or obstacles. The maps help pilots know where to fly and land. These maps change as the plane flies. They are connected to the Global Positioning System (GPS).

GPS uses information from satellites that orbit Earth. Each of these twenty-four satellites sits 12,625 feet (3,848 meters) above Earth's surface. These satellites can provide the location of just about anything on the planet.

In airplanes, a receiver collects information sent from the satellites. The receiver connects with a computer system and a monitor. The monitor shows a map with the airplane's location. Other

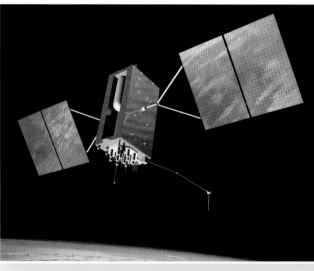

A GPS satellite (top) sends out signals from 12,625 feet (3,848 m) above Earth. An airplane receiver uses information from several satellites to map the plane's location (right).

information on the map includes the land below, the speed of the airplane, and the direction the airplane is moving. As the airplane moves, so does the map. It is constantly updated. A pilot always knows where the plane is positioned.

STAYING AIRBORNE: A BALANCING ACT

Flight is all about balancing forces. Thrust and lift keep airplanes in the air. An engine provides the thrust, a forward force. As the engine burns fuel, it shoots gases out toward the back of the plane. The powerful thrust pushes the plane forward.

Thrust fights against drag. Drag is the force created when a plane moves through air. Tiny parts in the air called molecules hit the airplane. That slows the airplane down. So the engine's thrust must be strong enough to fight the drag. The thrust keeps the plane moving forward through the air.

But how does the plane stay up? This is a balance between weight and lift. Gravity pulls down on the weight of a plane. But air can lift a plane up. The wings of a plane split the air's force. Some of the force goes above the wing, while some goes below. Wings are tilted up near the front and down near the rear. The forward edges are rounded as well. This guides equal amounts of air both under and over the wings. The air above the wings moves faster than the air below. It puts less pressure on the wings than the air below does. This causes the lift that keeps airplanes up in the sky.

An airplane's wings are designed to keep it in the air. Features on the wings guide air under and over the wings, creating a force called lift.

EARLY FLYING MACHINES

People have wanted to fly for centuries. But learning how to make machines that could fly took a long time. Many early inventors did not understand the science behind flight. They created some very strange flying machines, none of which could possibly work. Italian inventor Leonardo da Vinci sketched many designs for flying machines in the fifteenth century. The machines had flapping wings meant to be powered by a person's legs and arms. One failed 1670 design by an Italian priest was a flying ship *(right)*. It was a boat with a sail. Connected to it were four copper spheres emptied of air. The priest wrongly believed that those spheres would make the ship

SURVIVING A PLANE CRASH

Flying in airplanes is safer than driving. But when crashes happen, airplanes are ready for emergencies. Did you know airplane seats have features that help you survive?

During a crash, the force of gravity (G force) is really strong. It can make you feel dizzy and sick and even knock you out. If seats are not strong enough, this force can also pull them free from their tracks along the floor. Then the seats could break and tumble around the plane, smashing into other passengers in their seats. Many passengers could be hurt.

That's why airplane seats are designed to stay in place even when under a force sixteen times that of gravity (16G). Any force above 16G would most likely result in passenger deaths. Airplane seats are put through tests to simulate a crash. Crash test dummies sit in the seats. To come up with a good design, researchers look at how the dummies react during a crash. This helps designers make seats that reduce passenger spinal injuries. Designers also look at how well the seats stay attached to the floor. The strong 16G seats crumple to absorb much of the energy of the crash. This helps passengers stay conscious, and the design helps to prevent injury. Passengers can then quickly escape from the plane after it stops moving.

The people who design airplane seats use crash test dummies to try out safety features. The dummies show researchers how people's bodies would react to a real crash.

OCEAN SOUNDSCAPES

Above water, a ship's path may seem uninterrupted. But in the murky depths lie obstructions that could critically damage even the strongest of ships. It's important to "see" the ocean floor and any large creatures or icebergs ahead of ships. Sonar navigation systems let crews peer into the dark ocean using sound.

The sonar equipment produces a sound aimed in a certain direction. When the sound hits an object, that sound bounces back to the ship as an echo. Another part of the sonar equipment contains a receiver. This device gathers information about the echo, measuring how long it took for the sound to bounce back to the ship. Using the time measurement and the speed of sound in the ocean, the crew can understand how far away the object is from the ship.

Sound travels about 4,900 feet (1,500 m) per second in the ocean. So if an echo takes three seconds to bounce back, that means the sound traveled about 14,700 feet (4,480 m). The

A SHIP'S SONAR BEAM

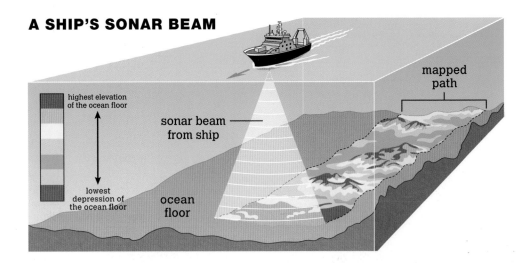

highest elevation
of the ocean floor

lowest
depression of
the ocean floor

sonar beam
from ship

ocean
floor

mapped
path

distance is then divided by two, since the sound first travels to the object and then travels back to the ship. The crew knows that the object is about 7,350 feet (2,240 m) away.

Computers mark many points of an area using sonar. Using the different measurements, they generate maps of ocean terrain. Scientists and a crew can use sonar to see marine life, deep canyons, underwater mountain ranges, and more.

MAYDAY, MAYDAY, MAYDAY! HELP AT SEA

Sail out to sea and you'll be miles from land and other people.
No cell phone towers are in sight. There's no Internet. And
there are no land markers to find a location. It's just you and
your boat between the waves and the blue sky. That can be very
peaceful. But if you're in trouble, you need a way to contact
help. If you are between 5 and 20 miles (8 to 32 kilometers) from
land, a very high frequency (VHF) marine radio is the answer.
This simple device is a boater's most important equipment.

All radios use radio waves. The waves are all around us.
You cannot see them, though. They are made of energy. This
energy travels from a source and spreads out as it goes. We
use radio waves to send all kinds of information—from music
to messages. Different radio waves have different frequencies.
Radio frequencies range from 10 kHz (10,000 sound waves per
second) to 100 GHz (100,000 sound waves per second). Certain
frequencies are reserved for marine communications. They
range from 156 MHz to
162.025 MHz (megahertz
equal one million cycles
per second).

When in trouble,
boaters send a Mayday
message on channel 16
of their radio. *Mayday* is
a word used by boaters

*If boaters get into trouble, they can use a
VHF radio like this one to call for help.*

worldwide that means they need help. The signal reaches a radio station on a coast guard ship or the coast. The boater states the exact location of the boat in latitude and longitude. It's a kind of global address. These numbers mark a spot on an invisible grid that people use to map the entire Earth. The boater also tells the station what is wrong.

The station can then call the nearest boat to help. It also sends a radio message back to the boater in distress. The boater listens on a different channel to receive the message. The station then tells the boater that help is coming.

The coast guard can receive distress calls and respond to boaters who signal for help.

THE POWER OF AIR

Stopping a train is not easy. If brakes fail, a runaway train can jump the tracks and barrel into a town. An average freight train has 90 to 120 cars. It can stretch over a mile (1.6 km) along the tracks. Train cars move forward at high speeds. This gives a train a lot of momentum, a forward-moving force. A large force is then needed to make a train stop.

What's strong enough to make a mile-long (1.6 km) train stop? Air! To be more specific, air pressure can create this stopping power. When air molecules are squeezed into a smaller space, the pressure increases. That means the air molecules have a lot of force. This force is used in a train's air brakes.

An air compressor squeezes air so it has more pressure. Each car has a separate compressor. This allows each car to brake at the same time. The air fills tanks that connect to a brake pipe. The brake pipe has high air pressure when the train is moving. To stop, the conductor pulls on the brake. That forces the air pressure into the brake pipe. This causes air to flow into a brake valve. The air then goes into a cylinder by the train's wheels. The air forces the cylinder to push pads against the wheels. The friction this causes then slows the train to a stop.

A train's brake system uses compressed air to create friction between the train's brake pads and its wheels.

THE FIRST BRAKES

Early trains from the nineteenth century had simple and not very reliable brakes. Brakemen used levers to press blocks against the train's wheels. Brakemen crawled atop trains from car to car to operate the levers. It took time to apply all the brakes to a train. The friction from the blocks very slowly stopped a train over a long distance. For example, a train with seven cars traveling at 28 miles (45 km) per hour needed 376 feet (115 m) to stop. In 1869, American inventor George Westinghouse invented the air brake. In 1893, US law required all trains to have air brakes.

Each car on a freight train has its own braking air compressor. That means that all the cars can brake at the same time.

RAIL AND WHEEL: A PERFECT FIT

A runaway train can lead to disaster. It can jump its track at high speeds and with heavy loads. Whatever it meets will likely be destroyed. Luckily, runaway trains are uncommon. That's because of wheel and rail designs. How the two meet is very important. Their shapes need to fit perfectly. This fit, along with friction and gravity, keep trains on tracks.

A train wheel is no ordinary wheel. It has a flange. This is the inner lip of the wheel. It sits inside the rail and angles up toward the track. Wheels make contact with the top parts of a rail.

Imagine cutting through a track. The shape from top to bottom is its profile. A rail's profile looks like a capital I. It has a foot at the bottom and a head at the top with a skinny middle in between. The rail is angled and shaped to fit a wheel's shape. The rail's top meets the wheel's flange and bottom. These are the points of contact.

Different forces keep a train on its track at these points. Gravity pushes the train down on the track. Friction also occurs at the contact points. This force is made when two things rub against each other. The right amount

TRAIN WHEELS ON THE RAILS

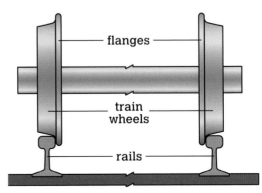

flanges

train wheels

rails

of friction helps train wheels grip the track. This is extra important when tracks curve. On a curve, forces push against one side of a train. This can cause lift on the side of the train along the inner part of a curve. On the outer part of the curve, the wheel's flange catches on the track. That helps guide the train safely around the turn.

Gravity and friction help to keep a train on its tracks, especially around curves.

SMOOTH GLIDING: MAGLEV TRAINS

While friction helps some trains grip tracks, it can slow trains down. Friction also causes wear and tear on rails and wheels. It's what makes a train noisy as well. So imagine a silent train that travels at super-high speeds. It hovers just above its track, never touching. This is not a train from the future. It's a maglev train. This kind of train uses magnetic force to race along its track.

Maglev trains exist in China, Japan, and South Korea. These trains hover above a magnetic field. This field is created with

Japan's HSST maglev train has been in service since 2005. This early demonstration model was used for testing and exhibitions in the 1980s and the 1990s.

magnets and electricity. All magnets have north and south poles. When like poles face each other, their forces repel each other. One type of maglev train uses this repelling force. Along its outside edges, the train has a cooled material called a superconductor. Along the track are wire coils charged with electricity. The electricity makes the coils magnetic. As the train runs along its track, the superconductors meet the magnetic coils. They create a current that lifts and pulls the train. The train hovers about an inch (2.5 centimeters) above the track and stays centered there. The train can move fast. Its average speed is around 250 miles (402 km) per hour.

By hovering, maglev trains do not create friction on the track. Without friction, maglev trains waste little energy. They are very efficient vehicles. They cost less than regular trains to operate. And they do not create air pollution, as fuel-burning trains do. This type of train is also very safe. Since the first use in 1984, there has been only one maglev train accident in which people were harmed.

EVOLVING SAFETY FEATURES

It takes years for good safety designs to evolve. Accidents that result from bad design lead to better design. Vehicles have become safer and safer as engineers better understand what happens during tragic events. New designs help vehicles crash more safely, absorbing energy that could harm humans. And personal safety devices, including seat belts and air bags, protect passengers from impact. These devices keep people from being badly hurt if a crash does occur, and they make it easier for us to get where we want to go. The next time you buckle up in your car, take a look at your seat belt. It's one of many safety features created by good design.

GLOSSARY

compressor: a device that squeezes or presses something, such as air, so that it will fit into a smaller space

flange: a guiding edge on a train wheel that helps it stay on a train rail

friction: a force that slows down two objects or materials when they rub against each other

gravity: the force that pulls objects toward Earth

latitude: the position of a place on Earth measured by its distance north or south of the equator

longitude: the position of a place on Earth measured by its distance east or west of a line that runs from the North Pole through Greenwich, England, to the South Pole

molecule: the smallest part of a substance that contains all the properties of that substance

momentum: the force or speed an object gains as it is moving

patent: a legal document that gives an inventor the rights to make or sell an invention

pressure: the force made by pressing on something

superconductor: a material that allows electricity to easily flow through it when the material is cooled to a certain temperature

SELECTED BIBLIOGRAPHY

Bibel, George. "The Physics of Disaster: An Exploration of Train Derailments." *Scientific American*, August 2, 2013. http://www.scientificamerican.com/article/the-physics-of-disaster/.

Bibel, George. *Train Wreck: The Forensics of Rail Disasters*. Baltimore: Johns Hopkins University Press, 2012.

Dalton, Stephen. *The Miracle of Flight*. Buffalo: Firefly Books, 1999.

Federal Aviation Administration. *Aviation Maintenance Technician Handbook—Airframe*. Oklahoma City: US Department of Transportation, Federal Aviation Administration, 2012.

"Radio Information for Boaters." US Department of Homeland Security. Accessed October 7, 2014. http://www.navcen.uscg.gov/?pageName=mtBoater.

LERNER

Expand learning beyond the printed book. Download free, complementary educational resources for this book from our website, www.lerneresource.com.

SOURCE

FURTHER INFORMATION

Discovery Channel: Maglev Train
http://www.discovery.com/tv-shows/other-shows/videos/extreme
-engineering-season-1-shorts-maglev-train
See maglev trains in action in this video.

DK. *The Train Book: The Definitive Visual History*. New York: DK, 2014.
Read this book to learn more about all kinds of trains—from steam to
high-speed trains.

DK. *Transportation*. New York: DK, 2012. Discover different kinds of
transportation, from jet engines to high-speed trains.

Eason, Sarah. *How Does a Car Work?* New York: Gareth Stevens, 2010. This book
explores the physics and engineering concepts that make car travel possible.

Lusted, Marcia Amidon. *Surviving Accidents and Crashes*. Minneapolis: Lerner
Publications, 2014. Learn about how people have survived different kinds of
accidents and crashes—from plane crashes to falling into sinkholes.

National Geographic—I Didn't Know That: Airbags
http://video.nationalgeographic.com/video/i-didnt-know-that/idkt-airbags
Watch how air bags quickly inflate.

National Geographic: Scientists "See" Ocean Floor via Sonar
http://video.nationalgeographic.com/video/news/us-ocean-floor-mapping-vin
Learn more about how scientists use sonar to map the ocean floor.

PBS Parents: The Wonder and Science of Flight
http://www.pbs.org/parents/adventures-in-learning/2014/09/the-wonder
-and-science-of-flight
Visit this website to try a flight experiment and learn more about how
airplanes stay airborne.

Waxman, Laura Hamilton. *Terrific Transportation Inventions*. Minneapolis:
Lerner Publications, 2014. Find out how different kinds of vehicles were
invented and the stories behind their invention.

INDEX

PHOTO ACKNOWLEDGMENTS

The images in this book are used with the permission of: © iStockphoto.com/ Sitikka, p. 1; © iStockphoto.com/lovleah, p. 5 (interview); © Richard Levine/ Alamy, p. 5 (newspapers); © iStockphoto.com/Katarina Gondova, pp. 6–7 (rainy road); © iStockphoto.com/haveblue, p. 7 (brake); © Bettmann/CORBIS, p. 8; © Photo Network/Alamy, p. 9; © Laura Westlund/Independent Picture Service, pp. 10, 18, 25 (diagram); © iStockphoto.com/wibofoto, p. 11 (car crash); AP Photo/Jon Freilich, p. 11 (Bela Barenyi); © World Wide History Archive/ Alamy, p. 12; © Dominik Spinski/Demotix/CORBIS, p. 13; © iStockphoto.com/ turb83, p. 15 (plane); © J.B. Spector/Museum of Science and Industry/agency/ Getty Images, p. 15 (early flying machine); © RGB Venture/SuperStock/Alamy, p. 17; © Blend Images/Alamy, p. 19; © Michael Hawkridge/Alamy, p. 20; © iStockphoto.com/enjoylife2, p. 21; © Brad Mitchell/Alamy, p. 22; © Robert Harding World Imagery/Alamy, p. 23 (train); © SuperStock/CORBIS, p. 23 (brakeman); © iStockphoto.com/Allison Achauer, p. 25 (train wheel); © G P Bowater/Alamy, pp. 26–27; © LWA/Dann Tardif/Getty Images, p. 28.

Front cover: © Caspar Benson/fStop Images/Getty Images.